Reflections OF A WONDERING MYSTIC

BOOK TWO

CONTEMPLATIONS INTO AWARENESS

Nadia G. Serry

Vancouver, BC, Canada

Dedication

To Life

To the searching hearts for a new path

A path that leads to mental and emotional safety

A path that teaches to recognize true love and harmony within our souls

…and in all forms of life around us

From one free spirit to another, Roksy, I am honoured to have our roads met. You are a unique, brave and gentle generous soul. May the sunshine always brighten your heart and your world.

Nadia Jerry

July, 2024

Acknowledgments

I would like to extend my sincere thanks and gratitude to Joseph Roberts, publisher and founder of *Common Ground Magazine* in Vancouver, for his invaluable input and insights; to Beth Emms, in Sechelt, for her dedication in reviewing the book with me, and to my genius graphic artist, Sara Cameron, for her professional work all the way from New Zealand, also for her patience and wonderful aesthetic eyes.

Contents

Prologue   1

Insights from Nature   3
    Loneliness Inspires Courage   5
    Communicating with Nature   16
    Whirling with Nature   19
    Time off for the Wind   21
    Nature's Act of Compassion   22
    The Loving Embrace of the Sun   23

Relationship with Self   25
    Elixir for Peace   27
    A Lesson from a Child in Dealing with the Past   28
    The Wisdom of Remembering the Past   29
    The Free Bird with the Broken Wings   31
    Pain, Peace & Gratitude   32
    For Your Soul's Sake   34
    Amazing Connections!   35
    Control or Intelligence   37
    Dedicated to Jennifer   38
    Hope   40
    Wasted Potentials   41
    The Limits of Inner Strength   42

A Moment of a Bold Truth	43
The Art of Living	44
Right to Left	45

Love — 49

The Vibration of Love	51
A Celebration of "True" Love	52
To Love or To Like	54
The Father or the Mother?	55
A Way of Being	56
Given in Love	57

Spiritual Practices — 59

Rituals	61
My Cat's Eyes	63

Spiritual Insights — 65

Only Eternity	67
Knowing "You" Comes First	68
Your Calling	70
Spiritual Growth	71
Let Your Soul Be the Master	72
A Message to My Dear Wise Women	73
Life, Purpose, and the Scale of Accomplishments	75
Holy Robes and Worldly Hearts	76
Inspired by a Quranic Verse	77

A Journey to Heaven	79
Heart with Wings	80
Divine Promise	81

Divine Love   83

My Red Rose	85
A Vacuum into Ecstasy	86
About Loneliness	87
White Fire	89
Queen Spirit	91
What Are You Waiting For?	93
A Prayer from My Heart	95
The Divine Breath in Your Heart	96
A Moment of Eternity	99

Epilogue	103
Notes	107
Biography	109

Introduction

Chaos and confusion prevailed.

Fatigue and stress captured our bodies and souls.

How can we find our way to certainty, hope and peace?

The search starts within…

Developing awareness of both worlds, the one around us and the one within us, is a good starting point.

Taking small steps to connect with our true selves will gift us with clarity.

Clarity will lead to understanding of the truth of our inner world.

Clarity and the knowledge of our unique nature will enable us to unveil a vision; a vision that eventually guides us on a path of renewed hope, comfort, and inner peace.

Realizing inner peace will create a space in our mind, heart, and soul, to connect with the natural world around us.

This marvellous connection is indeed a source of wisdom and enlightment.

The arts and skills of mindfulness and contemplation teach us about the harmony between our inner world and natural world around us.

Our ancestors, from various ancient civilizations and spiritual paths, left us a precious inheritance of the practical tools of mindfulness and contemplation that open the gates to the world of awareness.

The awareness of the presence of the *Divine* in all created things…

This awareness is the key to wisdom, knowledge, peace, and a safe existence during our perilous times.

Prologue

Coming Back to Safaga

Once again I returned to Safaga on the Red Sea coast in Egypt. My Book I, *"Reflections of Wondering Mystic: Learning to Trust in Safaga"*, revealed how our intimate relationship with nature leads to inner peace and wisdom.

Mental and emotional wellness is the outcome of inner peace, whereas wisdom gives us the knowledge and strength to understand and endure life challenges.

In this book I shared my contemplations into awareness that poured from my pen through my heart and soul. My observations about life, nature, and people, hopefully will help others to unveil their awareness around issues such as loneliness, confusion, pain, and suffering.

Awareness leads to awakening.

Awakening transforms lives, bringing understanding, tolerance, renewed hope, and inner peace.

May you find that special place of comfort and contentment in your hearts;

That special place that lies deep in the heart of hearts;

That special place that has been your gift from the *Divine* from pre-eternity to eternity!

Insights from Nature

Loneliness Inspires Courage

Since I spotted the Ibis[1] last year, hopping around the gardens of the resort[2], I developed a special fascination with this elegant graceful bird. Usually they start to migrate to this area later in the winter. However, the presence of a single Ibis delightfully surprised me this morning as it appeared earlier than expected.

Ibis is quite far from being a pet. Last year when I tried to take photos of a group of Ibis, I had to set out very early in the morning. They always come when it is quiet enough for them to enjoy the gardens with its palm trees, shrubs, and flowers. It was quite hard to take close-up photos since they are overly sensitive to human presence.

This morning I observed, with unique bewilderment, the movements and behaviour of that solo Ibis. I thought of his behaviour as a one-time show, however, it continued for three days. The Ibis behaved as if

---

1 Ibis is depicted in many ancient Egyptian wall murals and sculptures as it represented the god Toth, god of wisdom, knowledge and writing, and was considered the herald of the flood. It was of practical use to villagers as it helped to rid fish ponds of water snails that contained dangerous liver parasites.

2 It is Menaville Resort in Safaga, Red Sea, Egypt which was also the setting for book I. In 2016, Book I was entirely inspired and composed in the Resort. In 2018, many of the texts of Book II were inspired and composed there as well.

he was a pet that is familiar and comfortable with his environment. He approached people fearlessly and affectionately. He flew over railings of balconies and stayed for a while watching the far horizons. He hopped playfully on the beach chasing off the waves by the shore, and finally settled on the walk-way between the gardens and the beach. This allowed me to approach so near that I was able to take my dream close-up photo.

For the rest of the day I reflected on the mysterious behaviour of the solo Ibis. No one could explain to me its early arrival and how and why it arrived alone. What was more important to me was that this beautiful bird dealt with the state of loneliness by adapting to *and* adopting his environment.

The process must have included fear, doubt, hesitation, and even stress. Yet, somehow this intelligent being must have found enough courage to turn his unfortunate early arrival into an amazing adventure that brought him the attention, love, and joy that he missed from his own community.

Would you be willing to let Ibis teach you a lesson about dealing with loneliness? Are you willing to try to find the courage to venture into new experiences, new ideas, and even a new behaviour to deal with disappointments and life challenges?

The Charm of Co-existing

Three different lives entwined in perfect harmony: a growing tree, a middle-aged shrub, and a baby rose bush

How beautiful to watch such unity, such peace

No competition...

No insecurity...

No pushing for control or power...

No judgment, doubt, or fear...

No evaluation, prejudice, or scrutiny...

Just trust, compassion, and tender love

Together they are looking up towards the warm sunshine and the embracing blue sky

Together they are joyfully dancing to the tunes of life!

Quiet Passion

A few weeks ago, when I arrived here, the sea extended to me a sincere invitation to come and enjoy a happy safe daily swim. Shortly after, I felt that the sea started to like me. To my surprise, today the sea conveyed to me that he started to love me.

You ask me how? Well, he contained my whole being in a tender embrace. I enjoyed a feeling that I only experience during deep meditation whenever I am graced with the nearness of God; an embrace so gentle, so serene, so kind, and so warm.

Have you ever experienced a powerful passion yet deeply calm and quiet?

Lessons in Love from the Sea

What I adore about the Red Sea is its limitless deep blue water.

Water that glistens under the warm sun give us hope of love that will one day appear on the far away horizon.

Its kind tender embrace is not just warm and generous but it's also endless… eternal.

Stable and clear, yet mysterious, powerful, loving and gentle… a reminder of God's attributes.

The sea is our most loyal friend absorbing all our worries, giving us comfort and peace instead.

He transforms our sadness into joy, and heals our pain.

His most important attribute is that he will never ever change even during mighty storms.

He will always be the same stable, mighty, wise, loving friend even if you come to meet him each day with a different face.

Can we learn from the sea?

He can teach us about patience and stability even during the chaos of life, and how to offer our chest as a pillow of comfort to others who are in pain.

Fish of All Colours

Today fish of all colours surrounded me.

It seemed that they all agreed to include me in their joyful aqua party.

I observed with great admiration the harmony and spontaneity they all enjoy.

They all celebrate life without prejudice, judgment, or even awareness of the word "identity".

Yet they float together reflecting a strong sense of awareness of their own being and the presence of their environment.

The difference between the awareness of an "identity" and the awareness of "being" is the difference between slavery and freedom!

Perseverance or Independence?

Here, in the underwater habitat, I always see an environment where large groups of small fish live close to coral formations, sponge, sea weeds, and other sea animals. It seems to me they live as an interdependent community; they live in harmony and quiet understanding of boundaries and needs.

However, I have been noticing for a couple of weeks now, a solo bright fuchsia coral of about a foot in diameter, standing alone on its own mini island. The mini island does not expand more than the size of the solo coral. I haven't noticed any fish or any other sea life coming close to it.

I found myself wondering about the mystery of the solo coral day after day. What has forced her to separate as such from the group? What circumstances kept her away like this? I wondered whether her solo presence was a successful act of perseverance to survive, or if it was a brave declaration of independence. Most of all, I wondered whether this lovely coral was happy in her loneliness, or perhaps the love and companionship of the sea was enough for her.

A Happy Baby Dolphin

I blinked my eyes twice not believing that what I was watching was a playful baby dolphin.

Could he be brave enough to leave his mother and come so close to the beach?

Our beach is gifted with a few small under water islands of coral formations that house a variety of fish species.

Early morning, in the absence of the curious snorkelers, this brave baby dolphin dared to explore our area.

Was he lost? I doubted it, since he was happily jumping up in the air and diving again into the water.

He kept on circling and playing for a long while oblivious of his surroundings.

Obviously, he was not aware that his adventure had brought joy to my heart and a smile to my lips.

Indeed, the dolphin was my gift today!

The Ebb and Flow of Life

The time was three thirty in the afternoon. A gentle wind was dancing with the warm sunrays that penetrated the surface of the water, allowing me to see the seabed with amazing clarity.

I stopped moving and looked down, watching the perfect ripples of sand forming endless wavy lines. The distance between the lines was surprisingly equal. However, what caught my attention was the direction of the fine lines.

Well, despite the ebb and flow of the sea, the lines were pushed forward instead of backward. I wondered if the tide goes both ways, why the lines of sand were all facing forward rather than backward.

I thought this might be a new truth from the wealth of our natural laws. It may be offering us a lesson about our life on earth.

When we experience the ebb and flow of life, it seems that the natural process pushes us forward rather than backward. The wisdom here is to let go and keep moving with the flow, so our journey would take us to our desired destination.

Don't waste life energy in resisting the flow of life. If

you accept it willingly, whether what you experience is joy or hardship, the natural flow of life will push you forward to new beginnings, to new hope, to wisdom, and to peace.

Communicating with Nature

It's a windy day...

The sun is shyly hiding behind mother cloud.

Imitating the sun, regular swimmers are hiding away from the sea, seeking shelter from the cool powerful waves.

I hesitated a moment, then I decided to trust the invitation of the sea.

Indeed, the wind was never my friend, and at times I avoided the encounter with that mysterious strong being at all costs.

Today, I chose to trust the sea and I jumped in.

I talked my mind into sending to my body approving signals of the cold water.

I started to make my way through the grayish wavy water and then I stopped and looked up at the sky.

I asked the sun to grace us with a warm appearance.

To my great surprise, a couple of minutes later the sun left its hiding place and spread its warm rays, turning the water into the familiar crystal clear shades of turquoise.

I wondered at what happened and I moved in the water in a state of reflection.

Could it be possible that we can communicate with Nature?

Could it be possible that inter-communications exist in Nature?

I communicated with the sun and the sun communicated with the wind.

A few minutes later I enjoyed a calm breeze and a sparkling warm sea.

Whether it was a coincidence or not, the important thought here is that:

> when we experience a state of unity with Nature, during all its various moods;
>
> when we love it, whether it is happy or upset;
>
> when we honour, respect, and make peace with it;
>
> then, we will start to see it as a dear friend, and perhaps even become able to communicate with it.

Nowadays, and on a daily basis, people around the globe are terribly concerned about the weather. They stand outside of it rather than being part of it. They talk about it as if it is an alien. They worry about its force, its strength, and its unpredictable behaviour.

They forget that Nature's behaviour is a reaction to our own behaviour, our own separation from life around us.

Perhaps if we try to embrace Nature like a growing tender child, and be happy with it in all its various states; perhaps then we will be able to listen and respond to its cries of needs and suffering; and with time, Nature will make peace with us again.

I dream of that day when we all reach a state of peace and purity so that we qualify to co-exist and communicate with Nature as a dear cherished trusted friend.

Whirling with Nature

In my spiritual tradition[3], all created beings have their own way of glorifying the Creator of the universes.

Whirling is one way of glorifying our Creator.

People *and* Nature whirl as an expression of love and devotion.

Spontaneous whirling[4] is a state of awe and worship.

A few hundred years ago, scientific evidence proved that Nature whirls, whereas almost fifteen hundred years ago, Prophet Mohammad delivered this phenomenon as it was revealed in the Quran.

---

3 Sufism, also known as Tasawwuf, is mysticism in Islam. Sufism guides people to spiritual excellence. It is the station of Ihsan which the third level of Islam and it focuses on the purification of the heart and perfecting the manners of the individual, personally and socially. The first is Islam which presents the five fundamental pillars of the religion and the second is Iman which has six pillars.

4 The *whirling* was presented by Jalaluddin Rumi (1207-1273), a Muslim Sufi mystic and poet. A person, who reaches a deep state of meditation and love for God, would at times, experience the whirling spontaneously. However, later on during the times of Rumi's son as a Sufi master, it became a meditative performance that is taught according to certain rules. Only a minority of Sufis practices this tradition of meditation as it is not a core principle of Sufism.

The earth whirls, the planets whirl, the sun whirls, the wind whirls and the list goes on and on…

Indeed people attempt to whirl, however, when Nature whirls, it presents a magnum and the most powerful whirling you can ever imagine, faster than the speed of light.

It is powerful because it is pure…so pure; it is spontaneous and true.

Today I experienced a taste of the whirling sea.

I approached one of the coral islands where a swarm of fish greeted me and danced around me every day.

I felt the current moving me quietly yet surely in circles around the little coral island.

First I thought it was a one-time experience; yet I witnessed my relaxed body whirling several times with the sea and the fish!

I experienced a state of peace and ecstasy.

I wondered what else in Nature whirls in joy… tasting the divine presence?

Time off for the Wind

It seems that "Wind" decided to take some time off.

Today is the second day the wind flag has not been flapping endlessly throughout the day.

People around have been able to relax after the fatigue of the firm embrace of the wind that lasted for weeks. That strong being can show her love in a very mighty way.

As much as her love is appreciated, we were all cheerfully swimming and enjoying the calm sea.

We felt like children who were celebrating the absence of their dear firm teacher.

I made my way into the sea which felt so soft like silk and so smooth like velvet.

For today, our time playing with the waves was switched to a relaxing water meditation till "Wind" decides to end her vacation!

Nature's Act of Compassion

This morning I shed a few tears…..

It seemed to me that the sea heard about it and decided to cheer me up.

The sea negotiated with the wind and produced a gift for me.

A serene breeze spread over a beautifully calm sea.

I was thrilled with this gift and rushed to surrender my body to the deep blue water.

Since the waves took time off, the fish decided to surprise me with another gift.

A colourful group of small fish circled around me giving me cheerful company.

Soon enough my joy wiped the tears off my heart.

I thanked the sea, the wind, and the fish with a hearty big smile.

The Loving Embrace of the Sun

The past few days have been challenging. I felt exhausted, weak, and disheartened. This morning I had a chance to sit in the sun. I was on the sofa having breakfast when I felt the comforting heat patting my tired back.

To my surprise the penetrating warmth touched my heart and soul, not just my body. It was like the embrace of a kind old wise man who hugged a crying child in need of love.

God is Love! He knows how to reach us with tenderness and love, if it is not through others, then nature enthusiastically answers the call.

Relationship with Self

Elixir for Peace

It's because of the past that we are who we are today[5]

Accepting and embracing the past brings wisdom to the present

This wisdom creates a deep sense of compassion for us and others

It is a genuine compassion which is a secret elixir for eternal peace

Isn't this what each human soul is seeking?

---

5 This approach to dealing with and healing the past is a Sufi approach. It transforms the pain and suffering into a life force that inspires and motivates the person toward a positive peaceful life.

A Lesson from a Child in Dealing with the Past

A child loses his hold of the balloon string.

The balloon speeds up, floats away and disappears.

He couldn't possibly retrieve it and shed a few tears. He then shrugs his shoulders and goes on to find something new to satisfy his curiosity and cheer his heart.

This is a child's wisdom dealing with the past moment.

Once our past is gone, we can neither bring it back nor relive it.

Why spend our life and energy waiting for the impossible to happen?

Why defy the laws of nature?

Why choose stagnation and misery over a healthy flow of life and growth?

That child wiped his tears and moved on chasing a butterfly....

Would you be willing to try it?

The Wisdom of Remembering the Past

Well-intentioned people when they talk or write about dealing with the past, advise us to "forget" it or "erase" it.

I beg to differ!

I stand as an advocate for "letting go" of the past, which is a totally different approach.

There is a huge wisdom in not holding onto the past so that it will neither freeze our steps in the present, nor plant seeds of fear of the future.

There is also wisdom in being able to remember the past.

Remembering the health, happiness, or prosperity that we experienced in the past will become our hope in difficult times. That hope will give us the stamina and energy to go through, and deal with our present challenges.

When our hardships pass by with time, and we come to experience wellness, ease, or prosperity again; remembering our hard times will help us to appreciate the goodness in our lives. That goodness will be sweeter and more fragrant, thanks to our ability to remember the hard times.

Remembering the past can also provide us with valuable lessons and wisdom that would protect and guide us in our present and in our future.

If remembering the past was all bad, God would have not gifted us with our long-term memory.

There is a great wisdom in everything created in our universe; the secret is to know when and how to use it.

The Free Bird with the Broken Wings

I feel stuck…

Stuck, stuck, stuck…

Within your tight fist I play a game of freedom;

Yet the reality is that I am in your prison.

I pray to grow wings so I can fly free;

Yet you keep playing magic tricks to keep me from flying.

I feel helpless, hopeless, and heart-broken.

I scream in the darkness desperately trying to hold the warm hand of my spirit

I pray again…

Perhaps one day I will grow strong wings;

Yet until then, I will remain that free bird with the broken wings,

Stuck, stuck, stuck in the prison of your tight fist.

Pain, Peace & Gratitude

No one is born programmed to enjoy pain and suffering. Through life we try to protect ourselves as best as we can. However, we also know that pain and suffering is an inevitable fact of life. So can we transform our pain and suffering to become a healing potion?

If we are able to mix our pain and suffering with patience, trust, faith, gratitude, and stop fearing what "IS" right now; the result will be Abraham's paradise within Nimrod's fire[6].

The fire of pain and suffering will still be there but it will not burn who we are, and cannot touch our essence, our soul, our hope and our purity.

With these thoughts in mind, I laid down and closed my eyes.

To my surprise I could hear each and every cell of my body giving thanks to my Creator.

---

6 Abraham vs. Nimrod: Light vs. Darkness. A story mentioned in the Old Testament and also the Quran, the Muslim holy book.

I was able to witness how the energy generated by this state of meditation, started to heal each and every cell.

My physical and emotional pain started to loosen their grip on me.

Of course this was not an instant miracle but it's rather a process which the more we repeat, the more we experience healing taking place in our physical body, heart, and mind.

It is actually an exercise. Mind-body connection may heal or destroy; science tells you that[7]. It does not need any special gifts. However, engaging the heart and spirit in the process, would enhance the possibility of healing.

We are all capable of it!

Would you like to give it a try?

---

[7] This technique of Biofeedback with active positive visualization, and observation of breath, would enhance any course of treatment a person is undergoing. It is not a substitute to treatment except in cases of mild tension or stress.

For Your Soul's Sake

It has been almost two weeks since I was able to write and share my thoughts with you.

Being far from my pen taught me something precious......

Each time we take a moment to connect with our SELF through writing, painting, playing music, walking in nature, meditating, or in any other way we choose; our souls will be brushed with divine light.

If we succeed to connect with our souls each day, then soon the light that shines from within us will expand our hearts, comfort us and cheer the world around us.

If we don't make an effort to connect with our SELF, we will slowly lose this gift which is the source of our genuine joy, and soon the heaviness of the world will become our sole companion.

Are you able to treasure a few moments daily for only your soul's sake?

Amazing Connections!

For the past five weeks I have been patiently waiting for my body to give me a sign that it has started to relax. I have been trying everything possible to reach this target, following a rather demanding discipline of: sleeping early, swimming, walking in the fresh air, sitting in the sun, eating healthy, meditating, praying, connecting with people, connecting with nature, and connecting with my heart.

Today a marvellous sign took place leaving me in awe of the body's ability to establish amazing connections. I was sitting quietly in the sun absorbing its warmth, when suddenly I watched the fingers of one hand massaging the knuckles of the other hand. After a quick examination, I realized that truly the knuckles of my right hand were a bit stiff and needed attention. Usually my mind would be totally unaware of my body's needs till the silent requests become loud signals of pain or discomfort.

I was wonderfully surprised to witness how when we practice self-care, our body-mind connection works spontaneously and accurately. When we start caring for our being; when we start taking our life seriously enough to make time for self-care, our body-mind connection will be realized without having to learn about it from expensive and fancy workshops.

Sharp awareness and the state of being in the moment are gifts of a spontaneous body-mind connection. They are also two secrets of a successful life and a healthy existence.

Control or Intelligence

Don't let your body rule you, control you, or ride you.

Appoint your intelligence, wisdom, and discipline as the ruler.

If the horse of the ego takes control, the rider may end up over the cliff.

Your soul is the Master!

Your heart and mind are the indispensable executives.

Your body is the faithful follower.

Dedicated to Jennifer

It is said that when a newborn baby arrives to this world, it takes him or her a good forty days to adjust to our environment. Therefore, in a few cultures that have roots in old civilizations, a newborn is kept at home for forty days, exposed only to close family members, sheltered from the outside environment and crowds of people.

Years later, through my research into medical sciences, I understood the wisdom of this old tradition. After birth, it takes forty days for parts of the physiological system to be "complete". Spiritual science will tell you that it takes the soul that length of time to "settle" in the material world.

Today I experienced a taste of this! I sat on my balcony overlooking the deep blue sea while admiring the gorgeous bougainvilleas embracing the walls of the building in front me. I realized that I was not "here" yet. I counted the days since my arrival and they mounted to only 26 days. I visualized myself struggling to come out of what I left behind, just as the newborn's struggle to emerge from the darkness of the belly.

There is pain, fear, and hesitation. There is the separation from the familiar. There is the anxiety of being thrown into the unknown; the unknown that is already known to all those who were already here before me for a long time.

I heard "patience" calling me, asking me to be kind to myself. I paused, took a deep breath and reflected. I understood that the longer we stay confined, constricted, and limited in what we can do or experience, the longer it takes to adjust and be present in a new environment. All we can do is practice patience whether it is a new place, a new job, or a new relationship.

Trust time, trust our bodies, minds, and hearts; only then can we start to relax.

When we relax we will be able to see clearly and understand more. One day we will realize that we are actually enjoying a sense of comfort in our new environment, with all its peace in the midst of chaos.

Perhaps then we will be ready to welcome new experiences that will teach us precious lessons about ourselves and life around us.

Hope

Crying is a signal of the presence of hope in the human heart

The absence of tears lets sadness settle

And a hard shell starts to form in the heart chakra

Then the body and mind begin to move as if on auto-pilot

Ah! This may be an alarm signal for the absence of hope

And the beginning of a slow soul's death

Wasted Potentials

Many of us humans live a life of wasted potentials.

Please! Forgive me and put the resistance aside.

Wake up! Shake off the shadows.

Be brave and look into the deep clear water of divine truth.

Look inside; look around and listen to the answers of questions that matter.

Where did you come from?

Where are you going to?

Why are you here?

Be brave! Wake up!

Waste not more of your precious time…..

The Limits of Inner Strength

Many of us are able to draw on our inner strength to cope with life challenges. I witnessed those who use their inner strength to help others but are not able to use it as a self-help tool. I do understand the varied reasons behind that.

I also witnessed kind individuals who use their inner strength as a self-help tool; yet they are totally unable to use it to help others. I wondered why, and I am still thinking about it.

A Moment of a Bold Truth

A wise person loves all people without attachment.

Then what's the nature of attachment between a wise person and others?

SERVICE...

The service that you offer them is your attachment to them.

The difference between spiritual business and worldly business is that you get your rewards from God, not people.

A wise person offers perfect, just, courteous, compassionate service to all, under all circumstances, without judgment, nor expectations.

A wise person will also tell you that this way of living is the secret source of happiness, freedom and peace.

Only brave hearts are ready to do business with God!

The Art of Living

You are either living, or watching life passing by…

The true sense of feeling alive comes from being in an environment where you are able to contribute and receive joyfully.

The sense of spontaneous belonging is the essence of life.

So are you watching life passing by, or ready to find an environment where you are free to give and receive in a loving sincere way?

Right to Left

Yesterday I bought a notebook to jot down my thoughts whenever and wherever they come. I decided to carry this notebook with me everywhere.

I was surprised that unconsciously I opened it from the side facing right rather than left. Of course this was totally unintentional, and to me it didn't make sense. Next, I watched my hand starting to write from right to left. First, it didn't seem to me that it was an important matter; however, my inquisitive nature gave it a serious thought.

I shook my head as if to wake myself up and started to write "the usual way" from left to right. I felt worried when my feeling of awkwardness didn't leave me when my brain insisted on writing following the "opposite" way.

I grew up writing my mother language from right to left, and at the same time, French from left to right; and I enjoyed them both. Yet, today it was a very different feeling, a feeling of insistence towards one, yet resistance towards the other.

At the beginning I blamed this behaviour on my exhaustion from the long arduous trip coming from

Vancouver to Safaga. I thought my system was simply trying to attempt to adjust to a totally different climate, culture, and environment.

After careful and honest self-reflection, I realized that it was not just the trip but it was more than that. During the past eight months, back in Vancouver, I reached a stage where I surpassed the boundaries of exhaustion and fatigue; physically, mentally, and emotionally.

Then, I remembered the findings of a research I read about in neuropsycholinguistics. When the brain is fatigued or when we are under emotional stress, the brain will find it easier to resort to the chamber that belongs to the mother tongue, the first language we learned to speak, or to speak and write. Same point was proven not just for the spoken and written language but for math. Many people when they are fatigued or under stress, their mind counts in their mother tongue.

Only on the loving tender shores of the Red Sea I realized how much I was tired, exhausted, depleted, and wounded like a soldier who is trying to survive a lost battle. A soldier who is bouncing between defeat and hope; fighting for his soul, fighting for his life; watching sadly and fearfully defeat all around him in every corner.

Remembering the above noted research findings, I understood that my mind attempted to disconnect from my danger zone of exhaustion, seeking refuge in the land of my childhood. The peaceful reassuring shores of the Red Sea in Safaga reminded me of those early days when I ran to hide in my mom's lap for comfort and protection.

An afterthought note:

Years ago I watched a TV program where they mentioned that brain waves move from right to left. The presenter debated whether writing and reading while also moving the eyes from right to left, all in sync with the direction of the brain waves, is the secret behind accessing higher intelligence. He hypothesized that perhaps that would explain the greatness of a few of the old civilizations.

LOVE

The Vibration of Love

Would it be possible that the vibration of love enhances the beauty of whatever it touches?

From my own experience, I have come to believe that it is possible...

A fancy bouquet of flowers given as an act of duty may look gorgeous, however, a tiny hand-picked bouquet given from a sincere loving heart will not only look beautiful, but if you are able to listen to it, you will hear it singing tender magical tunes.

The vibrations of the gifts from a sincere heart, whether it is love, caring, compassion, or gratitude, will radiate eternal circles of joy and healing!

A Celebration of "True" Love

People around the world get anxious every year around Valentine's Day.

They believe it's a day to celebrate love. In their minds and on their agendas there are red roses, chocolates, candles, dinners, and other gifts to those whom they call loved ones.

In the frenzy of going around shopping for gifts and booking a table for two in the best restaurants, people forget that what we really need is true love.

The kind of love that is supposed to be practiced every day of the year; the kind of love that is supposed to be second nature to who we are, and how we live and communicate with one another.

If red roses are replaced with patience

If chocolates are replaced with kindness

If candles are replaced with forgiveness

If expensive dinners are replaced with respect

If all the other gifts are replaced with loyalty,
commitment, and the courage to communicate honestly

Our world will be celebrating love each and every day
and not only on Valentine's Day.

To Love or To Like

On February 14th while many people are celebrating the concept of love in its endless shapes and ways; I am reminded of a piece of wisdom given to us by my spiritual guide.

He said:

"To love humanity is a commitment to humanity.

To like others is a personal preference."

Once a person becomes spiritually mature and wise, it becomes clear how and why it is easy to love all people, yet not so easy to like all.

Not "to like" is not that harmful; but not to love can start wars.

The Father or the Mother?

When the wind calms down giving the sea a chance to give you a tender embrace, you don't know whether to thank the wind for calming down, or to thank the sea for the tender embrace that you have been waiting for.

Doesn't this remind you of the kind father with the bad temper and the loving mother who becomes too exhausted to express her love?

When the kind father controls his anger, giving the mother a chance to hug her children with relaxed tenderness, I wonder which one we should thank.

A child who grows up to become a wise compassionate adult, will tell you to thank and hug both: the kind father who wins over his ego, for even a short time, and the brave strong mother who succeeds to dive deep and gathers some genuine warmth and love to give to her children.

A Way of Being

No one owes me anything!

This thought is immensely freeing.

I owe life one thing:

to love everything.

Think about it…..

It is a sweet wise way of being!

Given in Love

What is truly given in love

    never

        gets

           less

Spiritual Practices

Rituals

Many attach the word rituals to religions and spiritual practices, yet they are prehistoric.

We know that from what was documented on the walls of the caves.

Humans came to earth with rituals as part of their innate nature.

Now people argue about the importance or the redundancy of rituals.

Many mock wedding celebrations, funerals, and ritual prayers but would fly miles to attend the Olympics inauguration or the Stanley Cup.

Many dismiss ritual prayers but wait anxiously for the yearly office party.

What they miss to notice is that those events are nothing but rituals.

I see rituals as a necessity!

They seal our intentions with a sense of commitment, a sense of purpose, and a sense of belonging.

What is your favourite ritual?

My Cat's Eyes

When I sit in a state of contemplation looking into my cat's eyes, I see a ray of eternity.

Animals have a transparent spiritual nature. They don't have the complex nature of humans nor their ego patterns.

Animals are innocent, pure, honest, and compassionate beings; therefore, they reflect a speck of the divine essence of life.

Animals, like all created things, glorify the Creator, constantly and under all life conditions, whether easy or challenging.

Unlike humans, they are intuitively and spontaneously in connection with the divine through glorification[8].

Humans can preserve their purity, innocence, and the ability to love through the practice of "Remembrance"[9]; to glorify and feel gratitude to our Creator and Sustainer.

---

8 Holy Quran: Surah An-Nur (The Light) 24:41 "do you not see that all those who are in the heavens and earth praise God, even the birds with wings outstretched? Each knows its [own way] of prayer and glorification: God has full knowledge of what they do."

9 Dhikr also spelled Zikr; Literally means "remembrance, reminder" or "mention, utterance". They are Islamic devotional acts, in which phrases or prayers are repeated. It can be done silently "Heart remembrance" or audibly.

Animals are our teachers in this respect, and should be respected, honoured and cared for, for this reason.

It is mentioned in the Holy Quran that all created things on earth and in heaven glorify the Creator. All have their particular way of glorification.

Let's rethink our understanding of Nature!

Let's follow in the steps of the saints and holy people who blessed the world with their divine wisdom throughout history.

Let's live our humanity before it's too late!

Spiritual Insights

Only Eternity

A flower falls off her stem; the wind comes to carry her away; she whirls and flies high over the neighbouring river, then the wind helps her to gently land on a nearby shrub.

Onlookers may see in this flower the end of a life cycle; yet the wise eyes witness the truth of eternity.

The divine wind that blew a soul into the first human became a symbol of the ever-present agent of life. At times the wind carries new life among elements of nature, yet it also helps nature to take new forms of being.

The wind is an eternal force that connects together all living things on earth. That fallen flower stayed alive when she was touched by the wind, and when was embraced by a hosting shrub.

Nothing that comes to life ever perishes!

To the wise eyes, all created things are eternal. We humans are created with love and that love gives us eternal existence. The norm for most people is to only see life and death; however, the wise eye only sees eternity.

Knowing "You" Comes First

"You have to believe in it in order to see it".

Thousands of meanings and insights stand behind that line…

However, try to believe today in "You" so you can start to see the real "You".

When you are able to see the real "You", the wisdom and secrets of the universe around you will start to become available to you.

"Why is that important?"

It is important!

How can you safely and successfully drive a vehicle while unaware of its capacity, its strength, and its weaknesses?

You will be taking a risk at each corner you turn, and reaching your destination will be left to chance.

So, how can you move forward in life safely and successfully without knowing "You" first?

"Where does one start?"

Ah! Learn the art of listening to your Heart so that you can start seeing the truth. When you start seeing it, you will be unlocking the first door towards your "Real Self"…

…and many other secrets you wish to unlock!

Your Calling

Do you expect to receive your calling without going through the "process "first?

Have you ever seen a pregnant woman receiving her child before carrying it?

Your calling is inside of YOU!

Yet, time, patience, perseverance, and awareness, are your prerequisites

Then, one day when you least expect it, your calling will leave the holy darkness, to the manifestations of light!

Spiritual Growth

Life presents us with learning opportunities to develop spiritual growth and strength.

It happens not when we think we are ready, but when God sees that we are ready.

We are not usually given what we believe we can handle, however, we are never given more than what we can *really* handle.

That is the nature of growth and rebirth. There is always discomfort and pain before the new experiences bring new levels of freedom.

I know you are strong enough to embrace the process.

Be mindful of food, movement, and breathing.

Be gentle with yourself, so life would be gentle with you.

Embrace yourself, so life is not shy to embrace you.

Let Your Soul Be the Master

I have come across people who love to speak about the "Truth", yet they don't want to hear it. Yesterday, someone got disappointed and even angry because I told her what she needed to hear, not what she wanted to hear.

This situation reminded me of our relationship with God.

We expect to receive what we think we need or want; and when we are given something different, or not given what we exactly expected, we get disappointed or angry with God and with life.

What we don't understand is that it is a blessing to be given what the soul asks for, and not what the ego wants. Soul's requests are true; however, the desires of the ego are misleading in most cases.

The soul works on a very subtle level, hidden from our conscious mind. If we let the soul be the boss, and not the ego, we will start to ask for the things that would lead us to our growth, happiness, prosperity, and wellness.

A Message to My Dear Wise Women[10]

You can't stand still on the seabed. Each time you try to anchor yourself, the gentle pressure of the water will uproot you and urges you to move and readjust.

The sea teaches us about our life out of the water. It is illusive to think or wish that once we settle in a situation, it will stay the same forever. Once we are done with one battle and victoriously establish roots somewhere, or with someone, life's natural law of ebb and flow will teach us that nothing remains the same.

We are in constant change; and it's wise to accept our ongoing challenges as opportunities that bring about transformation and new beginnings. Only then we will find enough life force to keep moving forward and upward.

However, we resist, we protest, we either express or harbour anger and resentment towards change; and the journey of transformation becomes harder or it stagnates.

Until we understand this particular natural law; until we have the courage to surrender and accept change,

---

10 Note: I developed "The Circle of Wise Women" in March 2016 until March 2020, when we had to stop the meetings due to COVID. I developed the circle to offer women of all ages an opportunity for spiritual development and a safe place for spiritual discourse.

the process of our progress will be enveloped in suffering instead of joy and growth.

Let the water of life carry you gently from one stage of life to another; be it one day or one year or more. Allow ease to be the theme of your life in whatever you do or whatever happens to you. You are wondering now how could you do this?

This approach is only possible when you become aware of your own resistance.

It is possible when you become willing to trust, surrender, and embrace the journey with all its challenges and unexpected victories.

The process will start to become easier to go through, and it will bring you happiness and satisfaction. Even if it turns out to be challenging or painful, you will gain new wisdom and strength.

You will win both ways!

Life, Purpose, and the Scale of Accomplishments

People look at old age with varied perspectives.

Many of us sink in a state of disappointment thinking that we have not accomplished anything meaningful in life.

We spend our wise years in circles of blame, sadness, and regret.

However, one of the secrets people do not know is that no one leaves this earth before accomplishing what they were destined for.

Divine Math is totally different from our human Math.

Perfection beams behind the imperfection; precision shines in the middle of chaos; and merciful love is disguised in the greatest failures, and the most horrifying events.

Holy Robes and Worldly Hearts

There are those who claim to be mystics and friends of God, yet their hearts are governed by other humans, or worldly engagements. The throne of their hearts is crowded by things other than just God.

A true mystic or a friend of God will not choose, at any cost, the dominion of humans, or anything else in the world, over their daily quiet time, hoping to be graced with the subtle yet powerful presence of God.

This precious encounter, if it is traded with anything else, the so called mystics or friends of God need to shed their holy robes.

Inspired by a Quranic Verse

From the Holy Quran – Surat Fussilat: Number 41

"Moreover, He comprehended in His design the sky, and it had been (as) smoke: He said to it and to the earth: Come ye together willingly or unwillingly. They said: We do come (together), in willing obedience." (11)

English Translation: Yusuf Ali

My Insights:

In contemplating this holy verse in relation to the human ego, we come to understand that the same divine law and the same divine order, applies to the human ego. It is an order that has roots in love and care. When the human ego refuses to bow down to divine law, it causes harm to itself and the world around it. Then the Almighty God will find ways to compel that ego to turn its compass towards the light and wisdom of the Truth. This happens by presenting hardships and life challenges for that ego to experience.

God presents these difficulties not out of oppression or punishment; on the contrary, there is great mercy and wisdom in this. If you understand the law of the ripple effect, then you will understand that the benefits of the divine "reprimand" is stemming from love and compassion that will ultimately benefit that soul, and that the benefits extend from that one soul to the rest of the universe.

If you succeed to protect one, you protect all, and if you succeed to love one, you love all.

Therefore, those who walk on the path of God in awareness will be able to see truth, love, light, and wisdom in life afflictions and hardships. Acceptance of life hardships enable them to find the strength to turn within and search for negative ego patterns or for wise answers to help them live safely through the challenges. This is the process of curing and freeing the heart[11] and consciousness from the ego's ailments.

Collectively, if this is done, then the world will avoid natural disasters and even wars.

> Let's not deflect anger and complaints towards the world around us, or in extreme cases, cut off our spiritual relations with The Almighty God.

---

[11] In Islam the heart refers to the spiritual heart, not the physical organ. It is this spiritual heart that contains the deeper intelligence and wisdom. It holds the Divine spark and is the place of gnosis and deep spiritual knowledge.

A Journey to Heaven

We heard and read about the ascension of Holy people to heaven both spiritually and physically. Indeed you must be a very special human being to be able to endure such an experience.

On a much smaller scale, you may experience, at least for a split of a second, journeying into heaven while you prostrate during prayers. If you are ready, heart and soul, you will be able to experience a flash, a tiny flash of that journey. That tiny flash goes deep enough into your being to elevate you high enough far from the troubles of your world.

Have you ever tried to prostrate in humbleness and gratitude to the Creator of the Universes?

Heart with Wings

Dedicated to the Hidden Spiritual Masters around the World

When your heart grows wings, you won't need to take a plane to visit holy places.

When your heart grows wings, you don't need to die and go to heaven to see the loving beautiful Face of God.

When your heart grows wings, there will be no more distance, no more time.

When your heart grows wings,

you will exist in the world of "BE" and behold! "IT IS".

Divine Promise

Do you think there is a correlation between the provisions you receive and hard work? Indeed, we need to work hard to earn a living; however, we need to be careful that in the process of earning an income, we don't lose our balance. One may work ceaselessly, yet at the end of the day will be faced with losses due to exhaustion of health or mind, or losing loved ones who felt neglected over the years.

In my spiritual tradition you receive what was ordained for you, however, you have to earn it too. Your internal compass will tell you when to strive and when it is time to stop. You need to be aligned with the Divine truth of life that will wisely direct your internal compass.

On the other hand, sometimes we receive without even working for it. The Almighty God, the Sustainer and Provider of the universes, is able to gift us with unexpected bounties. The world around us is full of endless examples of this phenomenon.

If we firmly believe that our provisions were ordained to us before we even arrived on this earth

If we understand that our duty is to seek a living through honest hard work

If we stay wise enough in order not to lose the work-life balance

What we will then lose is the unnecessary excessive fear, worry, and even paranoia that pressure us to stay in a toxic work environment or a destructive relationship.

There is also the concept of "Baraka", which means the blessings that protect whatever you receive. Have you noticed that some people earn modestly but their life goes on smoothly, and others earn ten times fold yet they are in constant need to make ends meet?

The secret here is gratitude and contentment, either you receive abundantly or you receive a little. That's what invites the Baraka into what you receive.

We are not alone! The Sustainer and Provider of all universes, who created us out of love, always takes care of our basic survival needs. The secret is to ask Him and believe in His generosity, love, compassion, and wisdom.

"Ask and you shall receive!" These words deliver a divine promise of a God who loves all without discrimination. It is up to us whether we activate the communication lines with Him or we live in fear of tomorrow.

DIVINE LOVE

My Red Rose[12]

When you sit in eternal silence

When life becomes a daily stare at dumb pieces of furniture around you

Escape into a prayer asking for the rose in your heart to be born again

Someone trustworthy told me that the Most Merciful listens to our whispers at dawn

Someone trustworthy told me that we are never really alone

Oh! My red rose how I wish to smell your divine fragrance again

---

12 The Red Rose in Sufism symbolizes Divine love and mystical experiences.

A Vacuum into Ecstasy

I always wondered why I have been lost in a vortex of suffering since my childhood!

Today God revealed to me that my Soul chose this particular path.

When we see, feel, and witness His *love* in each and every cell of the universe, we experience a *love* that would vacuum our soul into ecstasy, leaving nothing of our existence but ashes of joy.

This *love* renders anyone oblivious of any pain or sadness.

Not strong enough to experience this divine *love*; I retreat into my state of suffering!

I pray that my soul one day will find the courage to embrace this *love* as a permanent state, knowing that once you achieve, there will be no return to life the way you knew it before.

About Loneliness

If we are blessed by being in a beautiful place surrounded by things that comfort our mind, yet our heart cannot fully grasp the magic of the moment; it's because we may feel lonely or may feel like something important is missing in the middle of this bliss.

The truth is that we are totally oblivious of the fact that we are not alone; the One who granted us this special gift is with us, closer than our breath to us.

Have we ever thought that by feeling lonely while enjoying a gift of God is like brushing off the divine energy? That divine energy has the most powerful love to offer us, to fill our hearts and seal our experience with deep satisfaction. Yet, by being unaware of it, we put the divine song around us to mute.

On the other hand, we, humans, feel anguished when the person we reach out to with love is unaware of our presence, unaware of our love.

Therefore, it is a mistake to lose unawareness of the presence of the divine loving energy, while claiming loneliness and complaining about the "missing something".

The result is that this powerful healing loving energy shies away from us. We let the feeling of being loved, *that feeling that we are desperately looking for,* slip away easily.

White Fire

Love gives birth to longing

But my LOVE is still in hiding

Or is it me?

I am still a child learning to love the BELOVED

So, I fancy to be close to Him and to hug Him; and my wishes always end in frustration

When I start to dream of such nearness; I wake up to see myself running behind vanishing clouds

My listening friends, can you hear my pain, can you feel my loneliness?

I comfort myself with the scent of a red rose; I inhale the sweet scent with passion to taste His nearness

I hug the clouds with my eyes and refuse to let go to feel His nearness

I dive fiercely in the warm sea, then surrender and relax to listen to His nearness

Oh, what is this fire that burns incessantly in my heart?
I call it the White Fire of loving the Beloved

I wonder when and where this fire will be extinguished
by the long awaited-for Meeting

Would it be on earth or in heaven? Or perhaps in
another secret place….

Queen Spirit

I don't remember when it was the last time I felt like crying from the love I feel in my heart.

This time love is springing from a deep bright well in my soul.

A well that has been filling with His love for decades and lately the overflow of love and devotion caused pain and suffering.

Then one day, after what it felt like a million years, I woke up touched by His Grace.

At last I was blessed by what they call in my spiritual tradition the *"Divine Gaze" (Nazar)*. Nazar, or the Divine Gaze, is the love and protection of Allah the Almighty towards one person at a particular moment.

I experienced indescribable feelings of gratitude, humbleness, and joy.

Pure childish joy and enthusiasm overwhelmed my body, mind, and heart.

O life, witness this! Finally my soul has been crowned

the queen of my being.

No more supremacy for my mind, no more nagging from the body, no more doubts or fear in my heart.

Queen spirit stands in the Divine Court receiving and passing down to my mind, body and heart, gifts of guidance, love, discipline, certainty, and reassurance.

A bright eternal star has been assigned to light my *Way* now and forever.

What Are You Waiting For?

Love Him

for the sake

of

loving Him

knowing Him

getting closer to Him

Let go

Of

All

Expectations

Doubt

fear

Wait in faith

He will manifest His divine attributes in your heart and your life

Attributes of

beauty

love

abundance

peace

contentment

Enjoy and cherish each moment developing this incomparable liaison

What are you waiting for?

Don't you want to set yourself free?

A Prayer from My Heart

When I hear about someone in trouble, I pray to God from my heart.

Later, when I hear good news, I feel happy for the ease that came to that person, but more so ecstatic that He took note of my prayer, and pulled a heavenly cord to reassure me that He is so near, and I am part of His team.

Oh! How much I love you dear God…..

The Divine Breath in Your Heart

At the end it is just between you and God.

In fact all along it has been only between you and God.

At the end of your journey you don't take with you your gains or your losses.

What really matters is the transformations and the learning you accomplished on your *solo* journey.

What really matters is *who you are when you leave*, compared to how you were when you arrived.

Everything you do and everything that happens to you is nothing but:

> tunnels, bridges, mountains, forests, calm rivers and roaring oceans,
>
> *All*
>
> lead you through your journey to self-realization.

Self-realization is not about material success or gain; that is what you do for the survival of your physical being.

Self-realization is not even about reaching a certain spiritual station.

Self-realization is a state in which your heart reflects your unique beauty, hidden within your being.

Those reflections become rivers of love and compassion reaching all without prejudice.

You are able to see beauty in all and feel love for all, and your heart beats become divine tunes.

This is a state that is described in all the *Holy Scriptures* as the only gift accepted from us when we stand in the divine presence.

It is the gift of standing in the divine presence holding our pure heart on the palm of our hand at the end of our journey in this life.

So, dear friend, take time to be with yourself; be kind to yourself.

The service that you are longing to give to the universe should be given first to yourself.

Nurture and nourish the spark of the divine light within your heart.

Embrace the breath of the divine that resides in the secret heart[13] within your heart.

Then you will be sharing with the world each day the love, smiles, divine promises, and sweet hope that you heard about in the depths of your heart.

---

13 For detailed information check: A Study of the Term Sirr (Secret) in Sufi Lata'if Theories by Shigeru Kamada

A Moment of Eternity

You beg

You struggle

You collapse

You blow up

You then decide to let go

You then start to open up

You then learn to wait, and wait, and wait

Now you opened up

Now you are full of nothing

You are afraid to face chilled loneliness and haunting fears

You then call on your strength, on your faith

You ask the love inside you to sustain you, to give you hope

The journey continues…..

Till one day you think you went insane

Yet mysteriously you find the strength to move forward

To continue living with such courage that is foreign to you

You then decide to fly over all your challenges

And start to run against your fears, run and run, sweat and run

Suddenly, one day it happens in a flash of a moment, you calmly and spontaneously sit on the floor

Obliviously sipping a glass of water

Gazing at the afternoon sun

In a flash of that meditative serene moment

He enters…

He enters, and with bold conviction you know, with certainty you know, that He is now inside and will never leave

How? There is no how!

This was a gift from the space where no how and why exist

From now on He is inside; there is nothing bad or good that would make that presence leave again

It's a divine law!

Once that merge happens it's eternal, eternal, eternal

It's exhilarating!

You feel it in each cell, each breath

It's breathtaking!

It's life

It's joy

It's strength

It's health

It's safety

It's love

It's beauty

It's compassion

It's companionship

It's grace

It's peace

It's truth

It's GOD!

Epilogue

Permission

Everything enters with permission

Everything leaves with permission

Remember this……..and honour everything in between

NOTES

Nadia G. Serry is a clinical counsellor, career and diversity advisor, certified educator, and spiritual development coach. She combines a humanistic person-centered approach with cognitive behaviour therapy to guide others on their life journey.

She believes that we deeply heal when we find, or create, the right environment that meets our unique individual needs. Her preferred approach is bringing mindfulness and contemplation into our daily life in order to gain inner peace and wisdom.

Ms. Serry delivered workshops and participated in conferences in Vancouver, Toronto, and internationally.

To contact the author for sessions or coaching: ngserry18@gmail.com

Other Books by the author:

Reflections of a Wondering Mystic: Learning to Trust in Safaga

Hard copy and Online Version: https://tinyurl.com/yxd7w8gp

Manufactured by Amazon.ca
Bolton, ON

24067403R00074